Essential Events

THE KOREAN
WAR

Essential Events

THE KOREAN WAR

BY RICHARD REECE

Content Consultant
William W. Stueck, PhD
Department of History, University of Georgia

ABDO
Publishing Company

CREDITS

Published by ABDO Publishing Company, 8000 West 78th Street, Edina, Minnesota 55439. Copyright © 2011 by Abdo Consulting Group, Inc. International copyrights reserved in all countries. No part of this book may be reproduced in any form without written permission from the publisher. The Essential Library™ is a trademark and logo of ABDO Publishing Company.

Printed in the United States of America,
North Mankato, Minnesota
112010
012011

 THIS BOOK CONTAINS AT LEAST 10% RECYCLED MATERIALS.

Editor: Rebecca Rowell
Copy Editor: Paula Lewis
Interior Design and Production: Kazuko Collins
Cover Design: Kazuko Collins

Library of Congress Cataloging-in-Publication Data
Reece, Richard, 1948-
  The Korean War / by Richard Reece.
    p. cm. -- (Essential events)
  Includes bibliographical references and index.
  ISBN 978-1-61714-766-1
  1. Korean War, 1950-1953--Juvenile literature. 2. Korean War, 1950-1953--United States--Juvenile literature. I. Title.
  DS918.R428 2011
  951.904'2--dc22

                                    2010044661

TABLE OF CONTENTS

A South Korean solider rests on June 25, 1950, near the 38th parallel, while waiting to defend his country against the North Koreans.

TASK FORCE SMITH

On June 25, 1950, an estimated 100,000 North Korean soldiers crossed the 38th parallel—the division between North Korea and South Korea—and launched a surprise attack on South Korea. When word of the attack reached

Seoul, the South Korean capital located only
40 miles (64 km) south of the border, US advisers
there wired Washington DC. They informed US
President Harry Truman and his military leaders of
the invasion. The president knew the United States
had to take action.

Korea had been divided a few years earlier,
at the end of World War II (1939–1945). North
Korea was a Communist dictatorship. South Korea
was a fledgling democracy with a leader elected by
its people and recognized by the United Nations
(UN). The United States could not let communism
spread from North Korea to South Korea. With
approximately 80,000 military personnel in
nearby Japan, Truman and the United States risked
appearing weak if the US armed forces did not meet
this Communist aggression.

THE US RESPONSE

Washington responded by taking three steps.
First, President Truman ordered General Douglas
MacArthur to send material aid—not troops—to
the South Korean soldiers as soon as possible.
MacArthur was the highest-ranking US officer in the
Far East and the administrator of Japan following its

surrender in World War II. Second, the Air Force was sent to cover the evacuation of US citizens in South Korea. Third, the US Navy's Seventh Fleet moved into the waters between Taiwan and China, in case Communist forces invaded the island nation.

At the same time, the United States sought and received an official resolution from the UN that would allow the use of force to stop North Korean aggression. This meant the United States had broad support for its quest to save South Korea. It also meant the superpower would be assisting UN forces, not waging war merely to protect its own interests. The United States, officially, was not at war.

Meanwhile, the North Korean army continued to move south and overtook Seoul on June 27. In the first week of fighting, more than 34,000 South Korean soldiers—one-third of the army—were killed, captured, or missing. The only hope for South Korea was reinforcements.

On July 1, with UN approval, 403 US troops landed in the southern port of Pusan, South Korea. The soldiers were part of Task Force Smith, a mission named for Lieutenant Colonel Charles "Brad" Smith, the group's leader. The troops had been sent by MacArthur on 24 hours' notice from

Japan. The men had few details about whom they were about to fight and why.

When the task force arrived, Major General John H. Church minimized the danger when he told Smith, "We have a little action up here. All we need is some men who won't run when they see tanks."[1]

THE BATTLE OF OSAN

Two-thirds of the men in Task Force Smith had no combat experience. Most were younger than 21. Still, they were confident—

The United Nations

In the aftermath of both world wars, nations asked what could be done to prevent another war from occurring. After World War I (1914–1918), 58 nations formed the League of Nations in 1920 to create a body to settle disputes without military action. Instead, nations would discuss and negotiate and possibly use economic measures such as withholding trade. If all of these efforts failed, members would contribute forces to a peacekeeping army.

The United States never joined the League of Nations. President Woodrow Wilson had been one of its founders, but his political foes in the Senate blocked entry into the organization. The league failed to achieve its goal of maintaining peace in the 1930s when World War II erupted in Europe. In 1943, the delegates agreed to dissolve the league and create a new organization.

The United Nations (UN) formed in 1945 and met for the first time in 1946 with 51 nations represented, including the United States. The UN hoped to help members cooperate to achieve economic and social progress and to preserve world peace by providing a place where nations could express their needs and grievances. As of 2010, the UN had 192 members. While its effectiveness has, at times, been criticized, it is still a major platform for international dialogue and a vehicle for international aid and development.

World War II

The Korean War began five years after World War II ended—a war that entangled several nations and claimed 50 to 70 million lives. The two sides in World War II were known as the Allied forces and the Axis powers. Allied nations included France, Great Britain, the Soviet Union, and the United States, which became an active participant after Japan bombed Pearl Harbor, Hawaii, on December 7, 1941. Axis nations included Germany, Italy, and Japan. The war began when Germany invaded Poland. It ended with the surrender of Germany in the West in May and Japan in the East in September 1945.

perhaps even arrogant. Once they arrived at Pusan, the Americans were sent north. They traveled for three days until they closed in on the North Korean army 25 miles (40 km) south of Seoul. On two hills overlooking the main road near the village of Osan, they waited for the enemy. The position was good for an ambush— they could see the road going north for several miles.

The first Koreans the US troops spotted moving south were not enemy troops. They were peasants and South Korean soldiers running in terror. On July 5, around 7:00 a.m., the Americans spotted the first North Koreans. The soldiers from North Korea began their attack with tanks. This was followed by foot soldiers, more tanks, and then more soldiers.

When enemy tanks were within range, US troops fired with bazookas. But even when US artillery hit its targets, there was little damage. One observer likened the effect of the small US bazookas on the tanks to spitballs against armor.

The enemy tanks continued on the road right through the US position, firing as they passed. A few North Korean vehicles and tanks were disabled, but most simply bypassed the US contingent and headed south.

Next, the North Korean infantry swarmed past on both sides. At first, it appeared as though they were more interested in heading south than in surrounding the US troops. In reality, though, a portion of the North Korean infantry had formed a Y. They moved past the sides, or flanks, of the Americans. They then surrounded them, closing the branches of the Y, and attacked from behind.

It became clear very quickly that the Americans were sorely lacking in manpower, firepower, and battle experience. Approximately 20 US soldiers were killed in the first hour of fighting. Smith, who had commanded a battalion in World War II, realized the situation was hopeless. After three hours of desperate fighting, he ordered a retreat. But communications had been severed, and not everyone received the order. Some US troops stood and fought, while many shot until they ran out of ammunition before throwing down their weapons in panic and running away. Many of the Americans were killed or wounded during this ragged retreat.

By the next day, July 6, what was left of Task Force Smith's members—about half of the original force—joined US troops who had just arrived and were preparing to defend the next town to the south. Task Force Smith had failed to stop the North Korean army from advancing farther into South Korea. Over the next two days, the scene at Osan was repeated as the North Korean troops gained 36 miles (58 km) in 36 hours. Soon, more US soldiers arrived and joined the fight. Time and time again, however, they met a similar fate. ⌐

Task Force Smith Memorial

South Korea constructed a large memorial in Osan to commemorate the battle that introduced US soldiers to combat in the Korean conflict. The front of the memorial is lined with the flags of all the UN member nations that provided troops during the war.

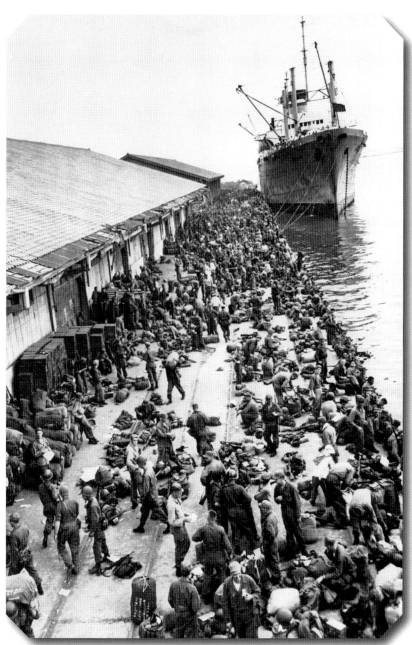

US troops arrived in Korea on August 14, 1950, to join outnumbered forces fighting to contain the Communist forces.

Chapter 2

Korea's division following World War II led to the Korean War.

WHY KOREA?

Korea is a peninsula in Asia that shares its western and part of its northern border with eastern China. A small part of the northern border is also shared with Russia. As a peninsula, most of Korea is surrounded by water: the Sea of

Japan to the east and the Yellow Sea to the west, which is connected to the East China Sea to the south by the Korea Strait. The distance between South Korea and Japan is about 120 miles (193 km).

Japan took over Korea in 1910 and did not rule gently. Historians often describe Japan's treatment of the Korean people as cruel and brutal. Over the years, thousands of Koreans were enslaved by the Japanese. During World War II, many Koreans were forced to fight, and died, for the Japanese. In addition, Koreans were not allowed to learn their own language, history, or geography, and they could pursue higher education only in certain fields.

When Japan was defeated at the end of World War II, troops from the Soviet Union and the United States accepted the surrender of Japanese soldiers in Korea—the Soviets in the North and the United States in the South. Following World War II, the Soviet Union and the United States emerged as the world's most powerful nations. The two superpowers had no desire to fight each other, and neither power really wanted Korea. But neither wanted the other to have it, so they divided Korea into two separate nations at 38 degrees north latitude—the 38th parallel. The Soviet Union would administer North

Korea, and the United States would administer South Korea.

Both nations hoped to unify Korea at some point, but they disagreed on how that unified nation would be governed. The Soviet Union wanted Korea to have a Communist government with a dictator chosen by the Soviets. The United States wanted Korea to be a democracy with a president friendly to the United States but chosen by the Korean people in a free election.

In 1948, the Soviets established a Communist dictatorship with

Communism and McCarthyism

Communism is a political system in which all the members of a group share equally in the work and profit of economic production. It was explained by Karl Marx, a German, in his 1867 book *Das Kapital*. Marx wrote that revolution would be the means to achieve a Communist society, and his works inspired the Communist Revolution in Russia in 1917.

To Americans in 1950, the word *communism* conjured images of the evil Soviet Union. Communism advocated the overthrow of capitalism, the free economic system on which the United States is based. For that reason, Americans considered communism, and even sympathizing with Communists, treasonous.

In 1950, Senator Joseph McCarthy of Wisconsin claimed to have a list of Communists holding positions in the US State Department. Although he was never able to prove this charge, it made him famous. Over the next three years, he dedicated himself to exposing Communists and Communist sympathizers in high places in the government, the military, and the entertainment industry. During this era known as McCarthyism, he and his committee destroyed the lives of countless Americans with unsubstantiated accusations of Communist sympathies.

Kim Il Sung as the leader. North Korea was named the Democratic People's Republic of Korea. South Korea was named the Republic of Korea. Elections were held in South Korea. Syngman Rhee, a strong anticommunist candidate favored by the United States, was elected president.

Many Koreans supported neither government. From their point of view, Korea was still occupied by foreign powers, just as it had been occupied by Japan. Sometimes, these Koreans rebelled. However, their uprisings were crushed, often violently.

ACHESON'S SPEECH

Neither Korean leader was content ruling half of a divided country. Both men dreamed of unifying Korea, and each man knew he needed help—permission, in fact—to do it. Naturally, Kim looked to the Soviets for help, while Rhee looked to the United States. But both powers had suffered economically and militarily

Last Name First, First Name Last

In Korea, it is customary to place the family name, or surname, first in a person's full name. For example, Kim Il Sung's family name is Kim and Syngman Rhee's family name is Syngman. Kim is referred to by his surname, but Rhee is referred to by his personal name. That is because Rhee spent many years in the West and follows Western practice, so he is known by the final name of his full name.

Kim's order to invade South Korea launched a war that would involve troops and medical personnel from several nations.

by the end of World War II—particularly the Soviet Union, which had been devastated. The last thing these powers wanted was more war. What resources the United States had were being poured into rebuilding Western Europe and Japan. The United States also drastically reduced its military forces to save money. The Soviet Union was struggling to consolidate its power in Eastern Europe and to improve its own floundering economy.

Initially, both powers left North and South Korea to fend for themselves—at least militarily. But the two halves were not equal. The Soviet Union trained and armed the North Korean army, turning it into an effective fighting force. By contrast, the United States left the South Korean army poorly trained and badly equipped for military action. The last US troops left South Korea in the summer of 1949. The following January, US Secretary of State Dean Acheson announced the defense line the US military would protect in the East, and it did not include Korea. Regarding Korea and other areas outside the defense line, he said:

> It must be clear that no person can guarantee these areas
> against military attack. . . . Should such an attack occur . . .
> the initial reliance must be on the people attacked to resist it

Kim Il Sung

Born in 1912, Kim Il Sung grew up under the oppressive colonial rule of Japan. He participated in revolutionary activities, joined the Chinese Communist Party, and became a leader in the armed guerilla struggle against the Japanese.

In World War II, he joined the Soviet army against the same enemy, and his reputation as a Korean patriot caught the Soviets' attention. When the Japanese were defeated, Soviet ruler Joseph Stalin installed Kim as a dependable leader of the northern half of Korea. Kim would lead North Korea until his death in 1994.

and then upon the commitments of the entire civilized world under the Charter of the United Nations.[1]

The speech was just what North Korea's Kim needed to spark his move to reunify Korea. The two Koreas were already engaged in skirmishes, with each side instigating fighting. The United States did not supply arms and other support in order to avoid a greater conflict. Kim convinced the Soviet Union that an invasion of South Korea would be successful. Shortly after Acheson's speech, Kim succeeded in obtaining Soviet support of the invasion by reassuring the Soviet Union of three things. First, he would win in just a few weeks. Second, he would use his own army. Third, the United States did not care enough about South Korea to get involved in its defense. Kim would be proven wrong on all counts.

Syngman Rhee

Syngman Rhee was born in Kaesong, Korea, in 1875. He studied at Princeton University and was awarded a PhD, becoming the first Korean to earn a doctoral degree from a US university. Rhee returned to his homeland, but he left again because he could not stand Japanese rule. He spent many years in Hawaii and then lived in Shanghai, China, and Washington DC before returning to Korea. As president of South Korea, Rhee was a harsh ruler who created a police state. He was intolerant of anyone who opposed him. Although Rhee had US backing, his leadership was far from democratic and did not support freedom. Rhee died in Hawaii in 1965.

Rhee became president of democratic South Korea with the support of
the US government, though his rule was not democratic.

Mao became a strong leader in the Communist world and provided North Korea substantial support in its effort to take over South Korea.

BACKS AGAINST THE SEA

With approval from the Soviet Union, Kim proceeded with his plan to take over South Korea. Meanwhile, a third party took interest in the Korean situation—North Korea's neighbor, China.

Mao Zedong was China's leader. He was also a Communist revolutionary and the head of the Chinese People's Liberation Army. Mao had led the army in a revolution against the nationalist government of China from 1927 to 1949. In October 1949, the army drove the nationalists to the island of Taiwan and established the People's Republic of China on the mainland. Both the nationalists in Taiwan and the Communists on the mainland considered themselves to represent the "true" China.

Although the nationalists in Taiwan still enjoyed millions of dollars in US aid and considered themselves the true Chinese government, the most populous nation in the world was, in fact, Communist. The United States was loyal to the old government, but the newly Communist China was too large to ignore. The United States

The Soviet Union

After the overthrow of Czar Nicholas II in 1917, the Russian empire broke into several independent republics. The Communists won control of the Russian Republic in a civil war and joined with the other republics to become the Soviet Union, or Union of Soviet Socialist Republics (USSR), in 1922. Eventually, all members of the USSR came under the central control of Joseph Stalin. During this time, Soviets faced strict rule, often through terror.

After World War II, the mutual distrust between the Soviet Union and the United States led to the Cold War, a period of tension and competition between the two powers during which each side feared the other would start a nuclear war. It lasted until the Soviet Union dissolved in 1991 due to political and economic difficulties.

hoped the nationalists and the Communists could share power in the Chinese government. But hatred between the "two Chinas" was deep, and far more Chinese people supported the Communists than the nationalists.

The Soviet Union had mixed views on China. While the Soviet Union supported China's Communist ideal, it distrusted China, fearing it could become a rival leader in world communism. The Soviet strategy was to appear friendly to China, but it withheld the kind of support—especially military—that could turn China into a superpower. If possible, just as it did with Korea, the Soviet Union hoped to use China against the United States without risking any of its own resources. When Kim first asked the Soviet Union for military help against South Korea, Soviet leader Joseph Stalin's reply was that Kim must get Mao's commitment to provide support if the United States intervened. Mao hated the United States for supporting the Chinese nationalists. Mao recognized North Korea's importance in keeping the United States away from China's borders. Kim obtained support from China and the Soviet Union. Stalin gave large amounts of weapons and military equipment to the North Koreans.

THE ATTACK

By 1950, small battles at the border between the two Koreas were common. South Korean spies had detected a buildup on the north side of the border since March. Roads were repaired, new troops and shipments of food and fuel arrived, and civilians were evacuated. This intelligence had been reported to MacArthur, but he ignored it.

Around 4:00 a.m. on June 25, 1950, South Korean troops along the entire length of the border were pounded with artillery and mortar fire. As they scrambled to respond, the soldiers farthest forward were literally run over by North Korean infantry divisions with more than 150 tanks and 1,700 large guns. The invasion was supported by approximately 200 ground-attack aircraft. Kim told his people the North Korean army had crossed the 38th parallel in response to a raid by soldiers from the south.

The South Koreans were outnumbered two to one. They had

President Truman

Vice President Harry S. Truman became president of the United States when Franklin Delano Roosevelt died in 1945. Only four months after coming into office, Truman made the decision to drop two atomic bombs on Japan to end World War II. He ran for president in 1948 and won. Truman did not run for reelection in 1952.

no air force, no real mortar or artillery guns, and no tanks. A massacre was in the making. Some South Korean soldiers made heroic—even suicidal—stands against the North Korean attack. Others, including some of the highest-ranking military officers, ran.

The first US reaction was denial. More than once, MacArthur had assured Washington that North Korea would not dare to fight for fear of an American response. He said the North Koreans were inferior soldiers and could easily be defeated. But tens of thousands of these troops had experience from fighting in China's civil war (1945–1949), and they manned North Korea's lead divisions. When the first reports of the attack came in, MacArthur dismissed the North Korean action as just another border incident. During a briefing on June 25, MacArthur said of the invasion, "This is probably only a reconnaissance-in-force. If Washington only will not hobble me, I can handle it with one arm tied behind my back."[1]

President Truman was in his Independence, Missouri, home when he learned of the invasion. He flew to Washington the next day and met with his closest advisers to determine how to respond. The invasion had caused officials in Washington to panic. Truman and his advisers had no way of knowing whether this was the latest chapter in the ongoing conflict between the two Korean nations or something worse. Perhaps the attack in Korea was planned by the Soviet Union to distract the United States from a Communist offensive in Europe or the Middle East.

Truman and his advisers agreed that the United States had to oppose the Communist attack, but they were not sure how best to proceed. Truman could order MacArthur to send weapons and equipment to help the South Koreans, but he could not send troops. The president could also act on his powers as commander in chief.

But there was another option. The North Korean invasion was a clear violation of the Charter of the United Nations, which had been formed to keep world peace. Within two days of the invasion, on June 27, the UN passed a resolution calling for North Korea to stop its attack

Allies in Korea

When the UN resolved to oppose the North Korean aggression, 16 countries contributed forces to the effort: the United States, the United Kingdom, Canada, Turkey, Australia, Thailand, the Philippines, France, Greece, New Zealand, the Netherlands, Colombia, Belgium, Ethiopia, South Africa, and Luxembourg. Some could muster only a battalion or a gunboat. Others contributed substantial numbers of troops. And countries such as Italy, India, Norway, Sweden, and Denmark provided medical support. All shared in the hardship and heroism of the war.

President Truman spoke to the American people about the Korean War and world conditions from the White House in 1950.

and return to the 38th parallel. It also called for all UN members to assist in enforcing this resolution. That meant US troops could fight in Korea under the UN flag.

Still, US lives would be at stake. To calm the fears of the American people, Truman held a news conference on June 29. He explained the situation, stating clearly, "We are not at war."[2] When pressed further, he explained why US troops were in South

Korea. During the conference, the term police action came up, and it would be used throughout the conflict. The transcript read:

> THE PRESIDENT. *The Republic of Korea [South Korea] . . . is a recognized government by the members of the United Nations. It was unlawfully attacked by . . . North Korea. The United Nations Security Council . . . asked the members to go to the relief of the Korean Republic [South Korea]. . . .*
>
> Q. *Mr. President, would it be correct, against your explanation, to call this a police action under the United Nations?*
>
> THE PRESIDENT. *Yes. That is exactly what it amounts to.*[3]

This implied that the country was not really at war and that the matter would be over quickly.

US airpower arrived first, bombing North Korean airfields and shooting down their planes. MacArthur flew into Korea to assess the situation. He advised that US ground troops were required immediately, and Washington sent approval within hours. US troops stationed in Japan mobilized for battle. The first of these troops to land in Korea, five days after the North Korean attack, were part of Task Force Smith.

The Battle of Osan was a disaster for the United States and United Nations Command. North Korea devastated the US troops. North Korea would not go away easily, quickly, or quietly. The war continued.

The Pusan Perimeter

As UN forces, primarily made up of Americans, scrambled to reinforce the troops fighting the North Koreans, MacArthur called for massive troop support—even the use of atomic bombs. He said an attack from the Chinese was likely to come at any time.

MacArthur also formed a plan to defeat the North Koreans. As reinforcements were sent to halt the North Korean advance, he diverted many of them to be available for his pet project. Meanwhile, US planes and artillery fought to slow down the North Korean army. A race was on between North Korean and UN forces. The North Koreans wanted to drive their enemy into the sea before substantial UN reinforcements arrived. The United States wanted to keep the North Koreans at bay as long as possible, anticipating those same reinforcements and more tanks, planes, and artillery. The UN forces fought and retreated, dug in for the next assault, then fought and retreated again. For weeks, the completely outnumbered UN forces fought and died to slow down the enemy.

By the end of July, the two sides reached a standoff. On August 1, UN forces established a defense line called the Pusan Perimeter. It enclosed a rectangular area around the southern port city of Pusan that measured 100 miles (161 km) long by 60 miles (97 km) wide. UN troops had their backs to the sea. The defense line stretched 140 miles

The Atomic Bomb

The atomic bomb was developed secretly in the early 1940s by a team of scientists working for the US Army. In 1945, Truman decided to use the atomic bomb on Japan to end World War II. By ending the war this way, he believed the United States would save tens of thousands of American lives that would be lost if the fighting continued. He authorized the dropping of nuclear bombs on the cities of Hiroshima and Nagasaki in September, and the horrifying result—more than 200,000 killed, mostly civilians—caused Japan to surrender.

Many Americans, even in Washington, believed that the atomic bomb gave the United States absolute power over any enemy. In 1949, however, the Soviet Union successfully tested its own nuclear bomb. After that, the threat of nuclear attack struck fear into both nations as each scrambled to build more and deadlier weapons.

Later in the Korean War, after China became the main US enemy, both MacArthur and Truman spoke of using the bomb against China. Mao was not concerned. "The Chinese people are not to be cowed by US atomic blackmail," he told one ambassador. "Our country has a population of 600 million and an area of 9,600,000 square kilometers [3,706,581 sq m]. The United States cannot annihilate the Chinese nation with its small stack of atom bombs."[4]

(225 km) along the perimeter from the Sea of Japan in the northeast to the Korea Strait west of Pusan. Much of the perimeter's western and northwestern border was formed by the wide, shallow Naktong River. Where the river turned east, it looped out to form an area called the Naktong Bulge.

During the fighting along the Naktong, the North Koreans frequently crossed the river using underwater bridges. They piled sandbags under the water and then used the stacked bags to walk across the river to attack at night. The bridges were covered in mud and impossible to spot from the air.

Battles of the Naktong Bulge

In August, the UN flew reinforcements and supplies into Pusan. UN forces repeatedly bombed the North Korean army on the other side of the Naktong when weather permitted. But the UN forces guarding the perimeter were in trouble. There simply were not enough men to form a tight defense. Companies of soldiers were spaced at great distances from one another. The North Koreans often made it through the gaps in the perimeter. And when attacks occurred, the UN forces could not come to each other's aid swiftly.

The situation for UN troops on the perimeter was incredibly tense. Every night, the North Koreans attacked somewhere along the perimeter. The perimeter often seemed like a giant sieve with the enemy leaking through each night. Not knowing just where the North Korean troops were at any given moment added to the frustration. For one month, attacks, bloody battles, and retreats occurred daily along the entire defensive line. While US troops knew they were somehow damaging the enemy, they did not know the extent of the damage.

The North Koreans fought to reach Yongsan, a village inside the perimeter. Whoever controlled Yongsan would control the area's main road. From there, the North Koreans could swiftly swarm south and take Pusan and capture the enemy or force them into the sea. UN forces, with US soldiers reinforced by US Marines, kept that from happening.

The Naktong Offensive

David Halberstam wrote about the Naktong Offensive in his article "Only a Few Came Home" for *Parade* magazine. He explained, "Those who survived understood in some elemental way that their unit had been sacrificed to buy time for others who might delay the North Korean drive. It was a hard thing for any soldier to accept—that in the cruelty of war he had been judged to be expendable. Yet somehow the strategy had worked: Although the North Koreans pushed forward some 10 miles [16 km], they failed to drive the Americans off the peninsula."[5]

General Walton Walker, commander of the Eighth US Army, worked tirelessly to strategically move his limited troops around in order to hold the line. Somehow, the Americans managed to stay in place through August, but they knew the North Koreans had massed their troops for a major assault.

That assault, the Naktong Offensive, came on the night of August 31. UN forces had done what they could to prepare, but they were overwhelmed. Charley Company, the US group farthest north, was practically demolished. Hundreds of US soldiers were killed, and many more—at least a few thousand—were wounded or missing. The orders from General Walker were clear and desperate: "Stand or die!"[6] And the Americans did just that. Every day, Walker wondered whether the time had come to fall back and set up a smaller, more easily defended perimeter. But two weeks after the initial attack, UN forces finally held off the enemy from the Pusan Perimeter. The tide of the war was about to turn. ⌒

The war had casualties of all ages. Many Korean children were made orphans. The US Air Force sponsored many orphanages.

*US marines head to shore during an amphibious assault
on Inchon on September 15, 1950.*

MacArthur's
Finest Hour

On September 15, 1950, approximately 70,000 UN troops landed at the port city of Inchon on the west coast of Korea, some 25 miles (40 km) southwest of Seoul, which had fallen to North Korea in June. The landing at

Inchon signified the realization of MacArthur's "pet project"—the plan for which he had set aside troops some two months earlier when US forces first went to battle in Korea. Early on, MacArthur had thought of launching an attack from Inchon because he believed the North Koreans would easily advance farther south. From Inchon, an army could attack the North Koreans from behind, putting them between enemy forces.

AN AMPHIBIOUS INVASION

The attack at Inchon became known as the Inchon Landing. An amphibious invasion, it required ships to carry troops, helicopters, and landing vehicles. These vehicles were equipped with wheels or tracks like those on tanks in order to travel on land once they neared the shore. To help clear the way for attack vehicles, gunboats and planes bombed the shore's defenses.

Operation Common Knowledge

For as much as MacArthur wanted the September 15 attack of Inchon to be a secret, that was not the case. Before the attack, the *New York Times* ran articles about the likelihood of an attack by the United States in which troops would infiltrate enemy lines. With the timing of the attack revealed, MacArthur and his staff focused on keeping the location secret. Then Japanese war correspondents also began discussing an upcoming US attack on North Korea. The reporters called the much-anticipated invasion Operation Common Knowledge.

To many experienced military men, this kind of invasion seemed too risky at Inchon. The channels that approached the shore were narrow and could easily have been set with mines. The tides were high and the current was strong, making ships and landing craft difficult to control. There were no large beaches, only piers and cliffs that would give the enemy's guns a great view of any invasion. And there was an island in the middle of the harbor that might be fortified with troops and guns.

Advisers noted that there were better places to attack closer to Pusan. But the riskiness of Inchon was part of MacArthur's strategy. He claimed the North Koreans would not expect an attack in such a place. He proved to be right.

THE LANDING

MacArthur watched the invasion unfold from the USS *Mount McKinley*.

Choosing an Amphibious Invasion

Perhaps the best-known amphibious invasion took place in World War II on June 6, 1944: D-day. On that day, Allied forces landed on the beaches of Normandy, France. It marked the end of German domination of Europe and the beginning of the end of the war. As a general in the Pacific during World War II, MacArthur had seen many such invasions as the Allies worked their way from island to island on the way to Japan.

MacArthur, seated, on the bridge of the USS Mount McKinley, *watched the assault on Inchon in September 1950.*

Ships bombarded the port, and the marines took the island in the harbor. Soon, 13,000 men stormed ashore and started advancing toward Seoul.

US forces used amphibious vehicles called DUKWs (pronounced ducks) to carry supplies from ships anchored offshore to troops on shore and to serve as general cargo carriers between the beach and the front lines.

The North Koreans were surprised, and they scrambled to send troops to stop the UN forces from reaching Seoul. MacArthur's plan called for the Eighth Army, now released from the Pusan Perimeter, to advance north and join the marines in the recapture of the South Korean capital.

However, that did not happen quickly enough for MacArthur, who had no idea of the obstacles facing what was left of Walker's troops. While MacArthur had lavished troops and technology on his brilliant secret project, the Eighth Army had, against great odds, kept the fight alive and survived. As the North Koreans headed north to stop the marines, the battle became as slow and bloody as previous ones.

THE TIDE TURNS

The tide seemed to be turning. The forces that came ashore at Inchon and those that followed were designated the Tenth Corps—X Corps—and put under the command of General Edward "Ned" Almond, one of MacArthur's favorite officers. Almond's first assignment was to take Seoul and meet up with the Eighth Army, which was to drive the North Koreans north. From Seoul, the two groups would continue the push toward China.

The UN forces arrived in Seoul on September 25, but it took three days of brutal fighting to defeat the

The Lucky Thirteen

Thirteen US Army nurses also landed at Inchon, including Chief Nurse Major Eunice Coleman. When fighting began, the nurses took cover in a ditch. "The whole sky was lit up by gunfire and burning vehicles," Coleman said. "About sun up we got out of the ditch and started treating the wounded. All that day we worked on the roadside operating and treating for shock. We lost eight men and a number of supply vehicles."[1] All thirteen women survived the ambush and began calling themselves "The Lucky Thirteen."

North Korean soldiers stationed there. Many of the North Korean troops retreated and escaped from the Pusan Perimeter, but as many as 125,000 North Korean soldiers were captured.

The US Army pushed the North Koreans back across the territory they had taken weeks earlier. Given the losses suffered and the purpose of the UN resolution—to stop North Korean aggression—it would have seemed logical for the UN troops to stop at the 38th parallel and negotiate a cease-fire. But they did not.

The UN forces were winning, and no one in power—in the United States or the UN—ordered MacArthur to stop the advance. All across the United States, politicians spoke of communism and the threat of it spreading worldwide. The public was anxious to see the Communists beaten back as far as possible. They also wanted revenge taken on the North Koreans for the brutality they had shown toward UN forces. MacArthur spoke openly of driving the North Koreans to the Yalu River, which formed North Korea's border with China. Although MacArthur mentioned it only privately, he dreamed of conquering communism in China as well.

China viewed the situation as a threat to its security. The Chinese made it clear that if the Americans threatened China's border, they would join with the North Koreans against the UN. But MacArthur and those in charge in Washington DC were not concerned about China's threat. The Soviets viewed the situation as an opportunity to keep the United States further tied up in Korea and sent more weapons to the North Koreans.

The US government did not want to risk another

Douglas MacArthur

Douglas MacArthur was the third son of a famous father: General Arthur MacArthur was a national hero, a military governor of the Philippines, and one of the highest-ranking members of the US Army in the early twentieth century. Douglas MacArthur surpassed his father's achievements, and his greatest supporter throughout his rise in the ranks was his mother.

Douglas MacArthur graduated first in his class at West Point, the US military academy in New York. He also served with distinction in World War I and was made a general at the age of 38, which is young for that position. As supreme commander of the Allied Forces in the Southwest Pacific during World War II, he became a media hero. After the war, as supreme commander of Allied Powers in occupied Japan, he helped that nation recover economically and rebuild after it had been devastated by two atomic bombs dropped by the United States.

MacArthur spent his adult life in the military, but he also had an active personal life. MacArthur married twice. His first marriage ended after six years. Eight years later, he married Jean Faircloth. The couple had a son, Arthur MacArthur IV. After the Korean War, and an unsuccessful bid for the Republican presidential nomination, MacArthur retired to New York. He died in 1964.

"By the time I arrived in Korea, the war had stabilized, which basically meant the enemy was on one side of the mountain and we on the other.

"During the day, everything was quiet but as sun set, the night sky would be bright with flares to mark enemy targets. Our unit would fight the entire night, and the next morning there would be a head count to determine how many men were lost during the night."[2]

—*William H. Warren Sr., Korean War veteran*

world war. But if the United States did not pursue the Communists farther north, the loudest opponents of the Truman administration would accuse it of being afraid of communism. On September 27, 1950, Truman gave an order to MacArthur—who still ruled the East from Tokyo and had never spent a night in Korea. MacArthur was to send his troops north across the 38th parallel, but to stop immediately if he was opposed by any Chinese or Soviet forces. No one who knew MacArthur would have bet on his following that order.

The view from a hill on the 38th parallel

North Koreans were held in a prison camp just outside Pyongyang during the Korean War.

THE ROAD TO A NIGHTMARE

n October 1, 1950, South Korean troops crossed the 38th parallel, leading the way for UN forces. Those forces crossed more than one week later, on October 9, with the plan to continue to the Yalu River. Five days later, Chinese troops began crossing the Yalu into North Korea to support the North Koreans. MacArthur headed his troops toward the border. Potential contact with Chinese troops would force him, according to his orders from Washington, to fall back.

Since Inchon, the general had been riding high. He expected the advance northward to be easy. He told his commanders that their men would be home for Christmas. He also told them to pack their dress uniforms for the victory parade in Tokyo that was soon to come.

On October 15, MacArthur met with President Truman on Wake Island in the Pacific Ocean. Truman disliked what he considered MacArthur's self-importance. Just before the conference, the president wrote to his cousin, "Have to talk to God's right hand tomorrow."[1] MacArthur had no respect for his commander in chief. He told an aide "that he [himself] was fighting the war."[2] He showed his lack of respect at the meeting by refusing to salute when the two men met. MacArthur resented anyone, even Truman, sharing in what he considered his personal glory.

When the president and his advisers asked about the progress of the war, MacArthur told them there was nothing to worry about. The United States knew that as many as 300,000 Chinese soldiers were organizing on the Chinese side of the river. Still, MacArthur was confident they were bluffing and would not dare to actually fight the Americans. MacArthur believed the Chinese had really taken a chance by fighting the mighty Americans and "that they now must be embarrassed by it."[3]

Most of the troops were optimistic as well. As they marched north, resistance was light. To some of the more

---

Winter: The Other Enemy

Veterans of the first year of the Korean War remember it as much for the cold as for the combat. The winter climate of Korea, unlike other parts of Asia such as Japan, is not tempered by the sea. Instead, it is open to cold air blowing straight down from the Arctic across northern China. The winter of 1950–1951 was one of the coldest in history. In Korea, temperatures were routinely −20 to −30 degrees Fahrenheit (−29 to −34°C). Blizzards often dropped several feet of snow on narrow mountain roads, making movement of troops nearly impossible.

In most cases, UN forces early in the war were not equipped with winter uniforms. Their vehicles and equipment were not prepared to function in frigid temperatures. Tanks and trucks would not start, guns jammed or cracked, and food froze. The army had rushed to the aid of the South Koreans in July and expected an easy victory. It had not anticipated remaining in Korea until the winter. Many would suffer frostbite or die from exposure. The Chinese, believing that Americans were unused to such extreme physical discomfort, used the climate to their advantage, luring the UN forces farther north as winter progressed.

experienced soldiers and officers, however, it felt almost too light. Also, they were spread out more, making them more vulnerable than they had been farther south. There was another concern. The weather was quickly getting very cold, and it was only October.

US soldiers captured the North Korean capital of Pyongyang on October 20. MacArthur flew in to congratulate the troops although he did not stay the night. During the celebrations, there was speculation as to how long it would be before everyone went home.

THE BATTLE OF UNSAN

Four days after the taking of Pyongyang, some South Korean units to the north, near the town of Unsan, came under heavy fire. They were slammed by mortar shells on the sides and from behind. This was a more skillful attack by a larger force than anything UN troops had encountered in weeks. The commander in charge believed it had to be the Chinese. Enemy soldiers who had been taken prisoner said they were members of the People's Liberation Army and had fought in the Chinese civil war.

The commander of UN troops sent word to his superior officer, who sent word to Tokyo. There, it was decided that the prisoners were probably lying. MacArthur ordered the UN troops to continue advancing. Then, on the night of November 1, approximately 20,000 Chinese soldiers struck at Unsan. Fighting ensued for the next three days. The UN forces were massacred. Those not killed or taken prisoner were driven back some 15 miles (24 km) to the other side of the Ch'ongch'on River. As the devastated and bewildered troops dug in and prepared for the possibility of another attack, there was no more talk of Christmas. Then, as quickly as they had come, the Chinese disappeared.

Pride Goes before a Fall

What happened next has been perceived as one of the greatest military mistakes ever. The powerful strike by the Chinese could have been

"[Some of my most vivid recollections of the war are:] The emotional highs and lows as the war ebbed and flowed. We were elated when we moved north toward the Yalu in November 1950 only to be fearful of the consequence of the overwhelming Chinese attacks that pushed us back to the 38th parallel. We hit a new high when Gen. Ridgway turned us back north from whence we had just come.

"Korea's 1950–51 bitterly cold winter also was near unbearable. We had not received arctic clothing because Gen. MacArthur had planned to have us home by Christmas. The clothing arrived in January and was 'warmly' received."[4]

—*Poise Lee Starkey, Korean War veteran*

seen as a warning, but MacArthur was unable to give up his dream of total victory. He believed the Chinese had withdrawn because they were exhausted and did not have the strength to continue. He reported to the UN Security Council that his men had killed or taken prisoner thousands of North Korean troops to date, and he would deal with any intervention from China just as severely.

On November 4, MacArthur ordered intense bombing on the Korean side of the Yalu River to cut off Chinese communication lines. Some of the bombs destroyed five North Korean power plants along the river. China already had at least 180,000 soldiers in Korea. But faced with continued aggression from the UN forces, the Chinese began to prepare their trap.

MacArthur's obvious eagerness to engage the Chinese despite orders to the contrary from the president made US allies nervous. The United States seemed to have little control over the general, and he

Power versus Knowledge

Although the UN forces were poorly equipped at the beginning of the war, the artillery and the air force eventually became their greatest advantages. Air power also kept the forces better supplied than the enemy. The enemy's greatest advantage seemed at first to be its numbers. However, MacArthur soon learned that the enemy's advantage was its knowledge of how to fight in the rough Korean terrain and how to exploit the confusion of those unfamiliar with it.

seemed to almost welcome what many feared would become World War III.

Truman and the army leadership were also increasingly distrustful of MacArthur. The general had snubbed his commander in chief at Wake Island. He had also withheld key facts from the president and some of the officers under his command so he could continue the war as he saw fit. When the fight had gone against him, MacArthur blamed the government for not giving him enough resources and tying his hands with restrictions about where, who, and when he could attack.

The job of a general is to carry out the military policy of a nation. To many in the US State Department, MacArthur seemed to be making and pursuing his own policy. Still, the general was incredibly popular with the US people. To relieve him of his post or to criticize him publicly would have caused serious political damage to the Truman administration.

During a break in the fighting in Korea, Private First Class Dwight Exe of the Fifth Cavalry Regiment wrote letters to send home.

*US tanks and jeeps filled with soldiers made
their way down a dusty road in Korea.*

MacArthur's Blindness

Not heeding the warning of Unsan,
MacArthur ordered the armies
forward. "Home by Christmas" was a phrase he
used frequently in talks with his commanders and
the media. General Almond's X Corps pushed

northward on the east side. Some of his widely separated forces reached the Yalu River on November 21, 1950. Marines under his command had settled around a reservoir near the west coast called Chosin.

After Unsan, General Walker's Eighth Army had consolidated troops around the Ch'ongch'on River. With UN forces positioned sparsely across the width of Korea and about 50 miles (80 km) from its northern border, MacArthur ordered them to attack on November 24. MacArthur ordered Walker to advance on the west side. But Walker, like many commanders on the field, believed MacArthur was blind to the dangers ahead. He also knew MacArthur did not respect him because he thought Walker was not aggressive enough. Expecting to be relieved of his command at any time, Walker moved his Eighth Army as slowly as he could without disobeying orders outright.

The Turkish Brigade

One of the most colorful groups among the UN forces was the Turkish Brigade. This group of approximately 5,000 young men with flowing mustaches and dressed in long, flapping over-coats carried swords that looked like long knives. The Turkish Brigade often fought in hand-to-hand combat, especially in the battles around Kunuri, North Korea, where they stalled the Chinese in subzero temperatures. The Turks eventually suffered more than 3,000 casualties.

The men in both armies had noticed that the farther north they moved, the colder and quieter it became. They knew the enemy was near. They seemed to be marching into a trap. They were about to learn that as many as 180,000 enemy soldiers were waiting in front of the Eighth Army, and an additional 120,000 soldiers were hiding in the mountains ahead of X Corps.

Kunuri

At 11:00 p.m. on November 25, the Chinese pounced. The first hit was against two companies at the northernmost point of the Eighth Army, which had considerably fewer men and less artillery. Approximately 4,000 infantrymen were killed, wounded, or captured. This loss did not help the marines, who were to begin their part of the offensive two days later.

The days went by, and the Chinese kept coming. Shock and fear spread through the retreating Eighth Army and casualties increased. Two days after the initial attack, Eighth Army forces tried to make a stand south of the Ch'ongch'on around the town of Kunuri, but they could see that Chinese resistance was collapsing. The enemy was driving back and encircling the Americans. Soon, retreat would be impossible.

On the morning of November 30, the army formed a long convoy to retreat on the only road south, which was their main supply line. There were rumors that the Chinese had already set up a roadblock. The army thought they would need to blast through with fast-moving tanks, trucks, and guns.

Soldiers were sent to clear out enemy shooters from the roadside. Instead, they discovered a nightmare.

Land Mines and Grenades

A land mine is an explosive device designed to injure or kill soldiers who are in the vicinity when it is detonated. Some land mines are buried and detonate when a soldier steps on a switch or trips a wire. One of these, the S1, was known in Korea as Bouncing Betty. When it was triggered, it launched and detonated at waist level. Other mines were detonated remotely by an operator upon seeing troops near the mine. During the Korean War, so many land mines were used that they remain a hazard. In 2010, heavy rains exposed mines from the Korean War era that killed one man and injured another in South Korea.

Grenades are small explosive devices that can be thrown by hand or launched by a rifle. Fragmentation grenades, sometimes called pineapple grenades because of their shape, were used extensively in Korea to injure soldiers who took shelter in trenches or foxholes. When the grenades exploded, the immediate area would be showered with sharp bits of metal. Concussion grenades exploded and created a shock wave that could stun and confuse soldiers. These were particularly useful against an enemy who was temporarily pinned down during a battle.

A Marine's Memory

James Brady, a US Marine who fought during the second winter in Korea, recalled his experience: "All of us . . . were haunted, whether we said so or not, by what had happened that first year, when . . . the Chinese . . . caught the Division at Chosin Reservoir and very nearly bagged them."[1]

At a place where the road narrowed between two high cliffs, a place they called the Pass, the Chinese had dug in. Sitting high above the road with heavy weapons, they rained ammunition down on the convoy as it tried to make it through the Pass. The road became clogged with bodies and disabled vehicles. At one point, the mechanical and human wreckage blocked the Pass entirely and brought the convoy to a halt. Soldiers jumped off vehicles to get through on foot. Some carried wounded comrades as the Chinese attacked from above with constant gunfire.

The US Air Force began to drive the enemy gunners from their positions above the road. A few soldiers attacked the hills and chased the enemy shooters back from the Pass. Late that night, the rest of the convoy passed through, and the Eighth Army staggered south.

CHOSIN

Eighty miles (129 km) east, in the high mountains, the Chinese had also laid a trap for the X Corps. Ordered to go all the way to the Yalu, the X Corps had been winding north. Temperatures were well below freezing, and the mountain roads were icy. Marines and infantry were marched around both sides of a manmade lake called Chosin Reservoir.

The Chinese, hiding in the mountains ahead, attacked the infantry first. The forward group of soldiers, under the command of Lieutenant Colonel Don Faith, was known as Task Force Faith. By the third day, it was demolished, and Faith was killed.

On the west side of the reservoir, the Chinese attacked the marines with mortars and waves of infantry attacks. Though they suffered terrible casualties, the marines fought off

"We have all read of the many unrecognized acts of Marine heroism during the retreat from the Chosin Reservoir.

"I was privileged to know first-hand of the courage of David Champagne. . . . In a shell hole with his fire team, an enemy grenade landed among the men. David picked up the grenade, throwing it away from the others. The grenade severed his hand and blew him out of the shell hole, where he was killed by enemy fire. . . . He did not live long enough to enjoy life as we have known it.

"We should never forget the sacrifices made by young men and women like David."[2]

—*Carl F. Ullrich,*
Korean War veteran

the enemy, holding their position and protecting their wounded. But the marines were surrounded; the Chinese had cut off their retreat. And retreat was just what they were supposed to do in this situation.

Still, the marines escaped Chosin Reservoir with all of their 600 wounded men on stretchers. The battle was every bit as dangerous, bloody, and full of sacrifice as any encounter in the Korean War. Faced with the results of the battles at Ch'ongch'on and Chosin, MacArthur had to acknowledge reality. The Eighth Army retreated to the 38th parallel, and the X Corps was evacuated and redeployed to South Korea. The great success of MacArthur's Inchon Landing had been overshadowed by his troops' latest losses.

US Marines rested in the snow after fighting in Chosin.

*British gun carriers passed an abandoned Soviet tank
on a demolished bridge at Osan.*

COMEBACK

By December 1950, the Eighth Army had
retreated across the 38th parallel and
reassembled in Seoul. The Chinese lined up north
of that position, preparing to attack. Despite their
losses, UN forces numbered almost 300,000 and

were still a match for the enemy. The experience in North Korea had taught them about fighting the Chinese.

The UN forces were well supplied with artillery and air power. Their communications were superior to the enemy. But the Chinese had used the terrain skillfully. They isolated and surprised parts of the UN forces, fighting at night to avoid air strikes and hiding from patrols during the day. The Chinese chose the battlegrounds. The Chinese were also experienced fighters as veterans of the Chinese civil war.

In contrast, the US Army had only a small number of veterans. Newer soldiers learned as they fought. Soldiers faced terror and pain. The horrifying experience at Kunuri had shattered the army's morale. The men no longer wanted to fight; many just wanted to go home.

But the UN and the United States had no plans to give up on South Korea. The strategy now was to hold a line north of Seoul, close to the 38th

The First War on Television

Television was invented before World War II, but television sets began being manufactured in great numbers only after the war. During World War II, audiences saw war footage in theaters—delayed by weeks or months—and presented in a cinema-like fashion and in groups. The Korean War was the first time people could see a war as it occurred and in a more solitary viewing experience on televisions in their own homes rather than in a theater as part of a group. This gave viewers a more personal, immediate feel of the war. It was happening live and in their homes.

parallel or as far north as possible until the Chinese and North Koreans were willing to negotiate a

peace agreement. But holding a line against the seemingly numberless Chinese was a terrifying prospect for many of the young and shell-shocked troops fighting as part of the UN forces.

Two days before Christmas, General Walker was killed in a jeep accident. On New Year's Eve, the Chinese struck the UN line north of Seoul. After four days of fighting, UN forces fell back. By the end of

---

The Military Code of Conduct

All US military personnel are to follow a code of conduct that they study as part of their training. It has six articles, which state, in part:

Article I: I am an American fighting in the forces that guard my country and our way of life, I am prepared to give my life in their defense.

Article II: I will never surrender of my own free will. . . .

Article III: If I am captured, I will continue to resist by all means available. I will make every effort to escape and aid others to escape. . . .

Article IV: If I become a prisoner of war . . . I will give no information or take part in any action which might be harmful to my comrades.

Article V: When questioned, should I become a prisoner of war, . . . I will make no oral or written statements disloyal to my country and its allies.

Article VI: I will never forget that I am an American fighting for freedom, responsible for my actions, and dedicated to the principles which made my country free. I will trust . . . in the United States of America.[1]

January 1951, the Eighth Army, reinforced by the
X Corps, had dug in approximately 75 miles
(121 km) south of Seoul, at the 37th parallel.

A Leader Arrives

General Matthew B. Ridgway was named as
Walker's replacement. He would change the war.
Ridgway was considered the brightest commander
in the army and brought confidence back to the US
troops in Korea. He did it by example and force of
character. When a soldier asked him what they were
fighting for, Ridgway replied,

> The real answer lies in the resolve of the free world to fight
> Communism, a regime in which men shot their prisoners,
> enslaved their citizens, and derided the dignity of man . . .
> which sought to displace the rule of law and to do away with
> the concept of God. [2]

Ridgway personally met every one of his officers
and removed those who seemed reluctant to attack
the Chinese. "There will be no more discussion of
retreat," he told his men. "We're going back!"[3]

Once the forces were in relatively more open
terrain, Ridgway outlined a new strategy. UN forces
would fight with its units close enough together to

US Marines questioned Korean women in North Korea during the Korean War.

help each other. They would use their vast artillery and air force to cause the most enemy casualties possible in every battle.

And UN forces had a better opportunity to wear down the enemy than they had before. The Chinese army was farther from home than it had been. UN air power had bombed Chinese supply lines, leaving soldiers hungry and cold. And many of the Chinese and North Korean soldiers who now faced UN forces were less experienced than the thousands who had already fallen in the campaign.

The UN Offensive

In early February 1951, UN forces began a counteroffensive to recover the 38th parallel. These forces occupied the villages of Chipyongni and Wonju and established a perimeter to protect the area before the Chinese unleashed their response. The Chinese sent huge numbers of troops, planning to encircle the UN forces and attack them from behind. Many Chinese troops were killed, but more kept coming. The UN soldiers holding Chipyongni saw their flanks fall back as the Chinese attempted to surround them, and the UN troops believed they could no longer hold their line.

UN troops fought desperately for almost three days to hold their position. Initially, the Chinese gained a hill and got through the line, but other UN units, especially the French, plugged the holes and helped keep the Chinese from advancing. Eventually, tanks and artillery rushed to help. When the situation seemed darkest, the air force arrived and decimated enemy soldiers.

After three days and nights of battle and staggering losses of men, the Chinese were exhausted. On February 14, they fell back to the north. It was the first major Chinese defeat of the

Female Veterans of Korea

Women also served in Korea. Many of them were nurses in the Army Nurse Corps. Some were part of the Red Cross. Still others were members of the US military. But the military had struggled to recruit women during World War II, and the challenge became even greater during the Korean War. The military did what it could to appeal to women to serve. According to the Women in Military Service for America Memorial Foundation, "To attract women recruits, the Department of Defense (DoD) launched a nationwide recruiting campaign including newspaper stories and media events glamorizing the image of women in the military."[4] Almost 50,000 US women served in active duty in Korea during the war.

war and a turning point for the UN troops. The troops who had been so demoralized following the horrors of Kunuri and Chosin now realized they could win.

UN forces continued moving slowly northward. They recaptured Seoul on March 18. By the end of the month, they were across the 38th parallel. The Chinese continued to attack, launching an offensive in late April. British forces fighting for the UN suffered greatly but hung on and proved successful. On May 16, 1951, approximately 137,000 Chinese and 38,000 North Koreans launched their last major offensive. The UN forces were prepared. The Chinese were massacred, and the Eighth Army again moved north. ⌐

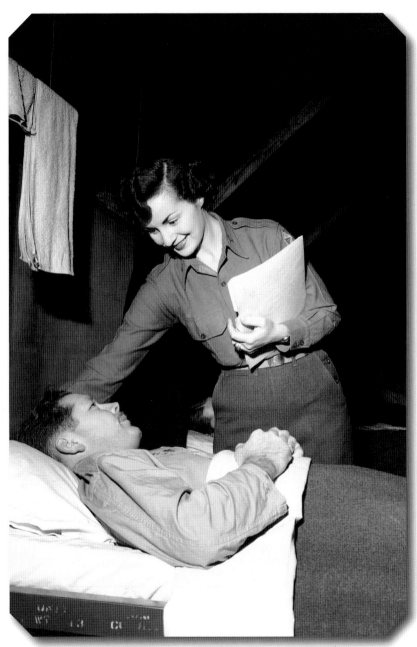

Thousands of women served as nurses in Korea and played a critical role in the war effort.

MacArthur, left, and Truman met on Wake Island in the Pacific on October 15, 1950, to discuss the war.

THE OLD SOLDIER RETURNS HOME

*I*n spring 1951, as UN forces successfully fought North Korean and Chinese forces, Truman considered MacArthur's fate. The president decided MacArthur had to go. The terrible defeats of the UN troops in late November 1950 were a result of MacArthur's unwillingness to face military facts. Even as the troops commanded by Ridgway began to show they could match the Chinese, MacArthur was calling for a wider war against Communist China and blaming the UN for not having the will to win his crusade. Polls showed that the US public believed him and blamed Truman's administration for keeping the general from proceeding.

Truman and his senior military advisers believed MacArthur's desire to bomb China would lead to war with the Soviet Union. This concern was even stronger among the US allies in Europe who already felt threatened by the Soviets and counted on US support to oppose them. MacArthur ignored their concerns. Although he had been ordered not to make statements about US policy, he kept doing just that. Some people thought MacArthur really wanted Truman to fire him, believing his own popularity would turn the public against the president.

As it became clear that the United States wanted the war in Korea to end more or less where it had started, with a country divided between communism and democracy at the 38th parallel, MacArthur's statements became more critical. On March 24, 1951, he publicly insulted China as "lacking the capacity to provide adequately many crucial items essential to the conduct of modern war."[1] This insulted the United States as well by implying that its failure to pursue further war against China was cowardly.

Truman had planned to make a speech seeking a peaceful settlement in Korea. MacArthur's remarks riled the public and forced the president to postpone that speech. The general's remarks also made it clear to the president that MacArthur was no longer a military asset and but an obstacle to his ability to govern.

A Soldier's Equipment

A US marine in the field carried a knapsack, a cartridge belt, a bayonet with scabbard, cooking equipment, a first-aid packet, a poncho, and a steel helmet with a liner and a camouflaged cover. In Korea, this was supplemented by cold weather gear: a parka with a fur-trimmed hood, mittens with trigger fingers, mitten inserts, waterproof pants, thermo boots, and heavy socks.

The basic shoulder weapon usually carried by UN infantry soldiers was the M1 semiautomatic. Developed in the 1930s, the M1 was gas operated, fired an eight-round clip, and weighed approximately ten pounds (4.5 kg). It could shoot accurately from 300 yards (274 m) and fire 30 rounds per minute.

In the field, soldiers ate C rations. Each box contained enough food for three meals for one person. These meals often included eggs and ham, pork and beans, or beef and beans. Sweets such as gum drops or cookies were also included. Soldiers also packed instant coffee, a tiny can of jam, a chocolate bar, and powdered milk.

The last straw came on April 5, when Joseph
W. Martin, a congressman friendly to MacArthur,
read a letter from the general on the floor of the
US House of Representatives. "If we lose the war to
Communism in Asia the fall of Europe is inevitable,
win it and Europe would most probably avoid war
and yet preserve freedom."[2] MacArthur was saying
the current US policy was a threat to the entire
world, including the United States' closest allies.

Fired!

Secretary of State Dean Acheson agreed that
MacArthur needed to be fired. But Acheson warned
the president that firing the general would result in
"the biggest fight of your administration."[3] Truman
expected he was right. But he had made up his
mind and would not take any more of the general's
insubordination. Truman sought the agreement of
his staff and senior military council, the Joint Chiefs
of Staff. It would be even more difficult to fire
MacArthur without the support of his most senior
colleagues.

On April 11, 1951, Truman addressed the
nation and stated that he was relieving MacArthur
as supreme commander because of differences

in policy. The president went on to explain that he was appointing General Ridgway to succeed MacArthur. Truman said,

> *A number of events have made it evident that General MacArthur did not agree with that policy. I have therefore considered it essential to relieve General MacArthur so that there would be no doubt or confusion as to the real purpose and aim of our policy.*

> *It was with the deepest personal regret that I found myself compelled to take this action. General MacArthur is one of our greatest military commanders. But the cause of world peace is more important than any individual.*

> *The change in commands in the Far East means no change whatever in the policy of the United States. We will carry on the fight in Korea with vigor and determination in an effort to bring the war to a speedy and successful conclusion.*[4]

In Japan, when the announcement was made, MacArthur took the news calmly. It did not come as a complete surprise. In the United States, the decision was extremely unpopular. Some called for MacArthur's immediate reinstatement; others called for Truman's impeachment. The most extreme accused the government of being controlled by the Soviet Union. MacArthur left Tokyo with his family and traveled to San Francisco. Crowds cheered MacArthur everywhere he went. In New York City, 7 million people turned out for a parade in his honor.

In Washington, the general gave an address to Congress in which he repeated his criticisms of the way the administration was conducting the war. He closed with these famous words:

> I am closing my 52 years of military service. When I joined the Army, even before the turn of the century, it was the fulfillment of all of my boyish hopes and dreams. The world has turned over many times since I took the oath at West Point, and the hopes and dreams have all since vanished, but I still remember the refrain of one of the most popular barracks ballads of that day which proclaimed most proudly that old soldiers never die; they just fade away. And like the old soldier of that ballad, I now close my military career and just fade away, an old soldier who tried to do his duty as God gave him the light to see that duty.[6]

Congressional Hearings

No one believed MacArthur was going to fade away. Many Republicans hoped he would be their next candidate for president in 1952. After his speech, however, the US Senate conducted hearings to find out just what had happened in the Korean War to date. MacArthur testified, as did members of Truman's staff, senior military officials, and officers who had fought in Korea. Americans heard Truman's side of events, including MacArthur's questionable tactics in withholding information and ignoring what he did not want to accept on the battlefield. Details of his disobedience to the president became public.

By the time the hearings closed in mid-June 1951, public opinion seemed to have a more balanced view of MacArthur. To many, he was, and would always be, a hero. But support for a MacArthur presidency had dissipated. By this time, the one-year anniversary of the war was nearing. And all parties seemed to be growing weary of war.

MacArthur, left, and Ridgway

Chinese troops challenged UN forces in Korea.

STALEMATE

y June 1951, China and the UN, with
the United States in the lead, said they
were willing to talk about peace. In July, fighting
temporarily scaled down. Military leaders from the
two sides met in Kaesong, in North Korean-held

territory, to negotiate an end to the war. When the meetings ended, fighting continued. The negotiations would take two years.

The UN troops had a limited objective. Their goal was to keep the enemy from advancing, to punish Communist soldiers if they tried, and to stay ready in case the talks failed. For the Chinese and North Koreans, the goal was to train new troops, maintain their line, and test the UN forces when the opportunity arose, all in an effort to move the line of demarcation back to the 38th parallel. In July, approximately 750,000 Chinese and North Korean soldiers looked across the line at 500,000 UN troops, which included 100,000 South Korean soldiers.

When full fighting resumed that month, it became a seesaw affair of capturing or losing hills and ridges, usually identified by numbers unless the newspapers named them

Recruiting

After World War II, the US government was pressured to reduce the size of its military. When men were suddenly needed for Korea, the branches of the military stepped up their recruiting efforts. During the Korean War, as many as 1.3 million men volunteered for the military, mostly in the US Air Force and the US Navy. To build up the army, the United States used the draft. The Selective Service Act of 1948 required all men ages 18 to 26 to register for mandatory service. They could be called for up to 21 months of active duty and five years of reserve duty service. Between 1950 and 1953, Selective Service inducted 1,681,862 men.

something more interesting. September brought the Battle of Bloody Ridge and the Battle of Heartbreak Ridge. No general offensive was authorized. UN forces fought in a limited way, but the killing was not limited.

In Kaesong, the talks started and stopped. The main participants walked out periodically over one offense or another. In October, the Communists agreed to switch the site of the talks to Panmunjom, a town in a neutral, demilitarized area straddling the border between North Korea and South Korea. November's talks consisted of wrangling about where the line between the sides would be located. The UN refused to accept the 38th parallel as an armistice line. Finally, a line was agreed upon that was essentially the line of battle, which was mostly north of the 38th parallel. Again, fighting scaled back. The Communists used the time to reinforce their defenses. Now, with a line agreed to by both sides, the UN pressed the

Casualties

In 1993, the US Defense Department stated that the Korean War resulted in 33,686 battle deaths among US troops, 2,830 non-battle deaths, and 17,730 civilian deaths. During the war, 8,142 US personnel were listed as Missing in Action (MIA). The total death toll, including all civilians and soldiers from UN nations and China, was more than 2 million.

US prisoners of war photographed in North Korea

Communists to sign a final peace agreement, but they declined.

Christmas 1951 came and went. UN forces and the American public grew increasingly frustrated. Ridgway let it be known that he wanted his commanders to do all they could to reduce casualties, but men kept fighting and dying while the peace talks dragged on.

Prisoners of War

By summer 1952, the negotiators at Panmunjom had agreed on a postwar line to be established between North Korea and South Korea at the line of battle. This was mostly north of the 38th parallel. Before a peace agreement could be signed, however, the sides needed to decide what to do with their prisoners of war (POWs).

The last obstacle to peace involved the more than 100,000 POWs from the Communist side. By some estimates, only two-thirds of these soldiers wanted to return to North Korea. However, the Communists insisted that all North Korean POWs be returned, claiming that many prisoners had been brainwashed against communism by their captors. POWs on both sides had been subjected to propaganda against their home countries and forms of government. But the UN held firm: prisoners who did not want to return to China or North Korea had a right to political asylum in South Korea or Taiwan.

The Communists were further embarrassed by the fact that they claimed to have only 11,000 POWs, which left thousands of Americans and 250,000 South Korean soldiers and civilians missing. In 1929, during the third UN Geneva Convention, the

Convention Relating to the Treatment of Prisoners of War established international rules regarding the treatment of POWs. The prisoners were to be treated humanely and their medical needs were to be met. Yet, there were widespread reports of execution, torture, and starvation in Communist POW camps. Often, as soldiers in the field had seen, prisoners taken in battle had simply been tied up and shot.

To deflect attention from this matter, the Communists in Panmunjom accused the UN of the very same tactics, including germ warfare. The sides deadlocked in October 1952 on the issue of returning POWs

Trench Warfare

The kind of fighting experienced by the UN forces during the lengthy negotiations in Panmunjom was familiar to veterans of World War I. In trench warfare, soldiers on both sides dug deep trenches and constructed bunkers to protect themselves from artillery. Then each side bombarded the other and hoped its firepower dominated.

This type of fighting is slow and often leads to a stalemate of battle lines and long waits, as the outcome might be decided simply by one side running out of supplies. At night, unless a battle is going on, men go on patrol, hoping to find enemy trenches into which they can shoot or lob grenades.

Because artillery and supplies were two areas in which the UN troops had an advantage, and because their goal during the peace talks was to hold the line rather than advance, this type of fighting suited them. When possible, soldiers in the trenches were rotated so they could return to a field base to bathe and get a warm meal.

A US soldier in a trench was forced to battle mud as well as the Chinese.

to North Korea against their will, and the UN
negotiators walked out.

Meanwhile, fighting continued. The
Communists became more aggressive, and
Americans died on hills with names such as Baldy,

Pork Chop, and Arrowhead. All this time, the position of the battle line barely changed. In the United States, General Dwight D. Eisenhower was elected president. Truman had not run for reelection.

The Last Days

In spring 1953, talks resumed at Panmunjom, and the fighting became bloodier. World public opinion was turning against the Communists on the POW question. In March, the UN proposed to North Korea's Kim that all wounded and sick POWs be exchanged at once. In April, the Communists proposed that POWs who did not wish to be returned to their home countries would be sent to a neutral country for a limited time to meet with representatives of their home countries. If, at the end of that time, they still did not wish to be returned, their cases would be decided by a conference formed after the armistice.

"My oldest brother, Cpl. Tom J. Mullins, was in the Army four years in the early [1950s].

"He was driving an Army tank when there was a "blackout;" his tank hit something, overturned, and caught fire. He was burned badly, [and] 190 pieces of flesh were grafted from his legs onto his back. It was a painful experience, but he never complained. Tom was happy to serve his country during the Korean conflict.

"Tom died in 1998. He was my hero. And I'm honored to be able to pay some tribute to him and the other veterans."[1]

—*Betty A. Williams, Chesapeake, Virginia*

The UN gave a counterproposal in late May that was accepted in June. But South Korean leader Rhee did not agree with the terms. By offering hundreds of millions of dollars in aid and food to South Korea, the United States finally encouraged Rhee to agree to a military pact and to not disrupt an armistice. On July 27, 1953, both sides of the conflict signed the armistice agreement. There were mixed feelings of relief, sadness, and puzzlement. It was hard to accept that so many lives had been lost in a draw.

South Korean troops waited in trenches to attack Chinese troops in 1953.

The armistice that ended the Korean War established a new dividing line between the Koreas. A South Korean guard stands at the demilitarized zone, facing North Korea.

THE FORGOTTEN WAR

The signing of the armistice agreement on July 27, 1953, finally brought three years of undeclared war and the sacrifice of thousands of men and women to an end. The Korean War was over. Many Americans hardly seemed to notice.

To those who did, it seemed that nothing had been accomplished—the border between North Korea and South Korea remained the same as before the war.

Following the Armistice in 1953, the UN created the Demilitarized Zone (DMZ). This strip of land is 2.5 miles (4 km) wide and crosses the 38th parallel at an angle. The west end of the DMZ lies south of the parallel; the east end lies north of it. Most of the line is in North Korea. In the armistice, both sides agreed to move their troops back a little more than one mile (1.6 km) from the front line, creating a buffer zone.

The DMZ Today

Because of continued hostility between North and South Korea, a large number of troops are still stationed along both sides of the DMZ. The troops guard against aggression from the other side and prevent individuals from crossing the border illegally. Isolated incidents of shots being fired occurred as recently as 2009. Since the war, more than 500 South Korean soldiers and 50 US soldiers have been killed in these incidents.

Despite the danger, there are guided tours of the DMZ. Most take visitors to an observatory and into Panmunjom where the peace talks in 1951 and 1952 took place.

A DIFFERENT WORLD

Korea appeared the same from a distance, but the world had become more complicated for the United States. War had lost its glamour. US veterans returning home from Korea remembered the large parades in towns across the United States for the men returning from World War II. But these newest veterans had a different experience. The nation that had held its breath while Germany and Japan threatened the world was now interested in raising families, making money, and having a good time. Still, the war helped shift US attention to the Far East, an area that would become increasingly important over time.

Korea had been sold as a war against communism. If that was its purpose, it felt like a failure to many Americans and the US government. Communism

The Two Koreas Today

Since the war, South Korea has become a prosperous democracy. Its economy depends heavily on international trade. While South Korea has significantly enhanced its defense capability, approximately 28,500 US military personnel are stationed throughout the country.

As of 2010, North Korea remained under Communist rule. Dictator Kim Jong Il, son of Kim Il Sung, ruled the country. North Korea may be the most isolated nation in the world. The government tightly controls information leaving or entering the country. A famine from 1995 to 1997 is believed to have killed 1 to 2 million people. North Korea's economy is almost stagnant. International trade is highly restricted. The state provides free food rations, housing, health care, and education.

The dream of a reunified Korea lives on in the hearts of many Koreans on both sides of the border. But for 60 years, relations between the two nations have veered between attempts at cooperation and overt hostility. In May 2010, after being accused by South Korea of sinking one of its ships, North Korea broke off diplomatic relations with its neighbor. In November, North Korea attacked a civilian area of South Korea with artillery. It was the first such attack since the war. The action killed four South Koreans and increased tensions in the region.

seemed stronger than ever. The Soviet Union and the United States were engaged in a race to see which nation could create more and better weapons of mass destruction. Some thought perhaps MacArthur was right. Maybe the United States should have taken on China. For China, the Korean War had been a boost. Despite the result, China was now recognized by the world as a power to be reckoned with.

LIMITED WAR

The United States had also had its first taste of "limited" war. Korea had shown that such a war could be easy to get into but highly difficult to get out of. The United States had gone into Korea not to defeat a threat or to recover stolen territory or even to help an ally. South Korea really meant little to the United States in and of itself.

The United States had entered the Korean War to prevent a political problem. The world was becoming

Communism in the Twenty-First Century

In 2010, there were five Communist states in the world: China, Cuba, Laos, North Korea, and Vietnam. There are also several democratic countries where the Communist Party is a significant participant in the government, including France, South Africa, and India. In the twentieth century, rulers such as Stalin and Mao judged each other on the "purity" of their communism. It was determined by how closely they followed what they saw as the teachings of Karl Marx. But "pure" communism, as applied to national economies in the Soviet Union and China, failed. In order to improve the standard of living of their people, even nominally Communist countries have made accommodations to capitalism.

a chess game between the United States and the Soviet Union. The atomic age had made defeating communism too dangerous, so the United States would strive in the coming years to contain it, to keep it surrounded by democratic nations that were friendly to the United States. But it would be difficult to ask Americans to die in a war that seemed so vague and whose end result was so undefined.

The Korean War Veterans Memorial

In 1992, President George H. W. Bush broke ground for the Korean War Veterans Memorial in Washington DC. It was dedicated in 1995 by President Bill Clinton and Kim Young Sam, president of South Korea. Within the memorial's black granite triangular walls are 19 stainless steel statues representing a squad on patrol. Fourteen of the figures are from the US Army, three are from the US Marine Corps, one is a US Navy Corpsman, and one is a US Air Force Forward Air Observer. The message "Freedom Is Not Free" is inscribed on an inside wall.

Unsung Heroes

Although the Korean War resulted in the deaths of more than 2 million people, it is referred to in the United States today as the Forgotten War. World War II and other wars have been the topics of many more books and movies than the Korean War. It is often given only brief consideration in history classes. Memorable wars have a beginning, famous heroes, and a dramatic end. Korea had a beginning, but its heroes are mostly anonymous.

Approximately 5.7 million Americans served in the Korean War.

In June 2010, Korean War veterans visited a war monument in South Korea in honor of the sixtieth anniversary of the war. Some were among the troops who fought in the Pusan Perimeter.

In 2008, more than 3 million were still living. Many remember the hardships of the war, the deaths of comrades, and the disappointment on returning home and discovering that no one seemed to care. Memorials in 2010 marked the war's sixtieth anniversary. Jack Lloyd Wallace of North Carolina recalled the occasion:

> *Later in the summer of 1953, the armistice was signed and we were discharged from the Army. I was formally*

discharged in Fort Jackson, [South Carolina]. Without a phone call home to my parents, I took a bus to Raleigh and then another to Washington, [North Carolina]. I arrived around 2 a.m. and had to walk the remaining 15 miles [24 km] to my home in Bath.

There were no banners, no songs, and no reception. Most people didn't even realize the war was over.[1]

Arthur Hiscock, a Canadian veteran, also shared in the experience of feeling forgotten as a vet. He explained:

It has been an ongoing battle to earn recognition. It took 40 years to get recognition that it was a war. A lot of soldiers died during that time and never got the recognition they deserved.[2]

Still No Peace Agreement

When South Korea's president agreed to the armistice, he was not agreeing to a final peace agreement, only to ending the war. As of 2010, South Korea had not yet signed the peace agreement ending the war.

For the men and women who served in the Korean War, perhaps the one place their memory will flourish is in South Korea itself. That country stands in sharp contrast to its northern neighbor in terms of prosperity and personal freedom. The Korean War helped preserve a place where that life became possible.

Statues of the Korean War Veterans Memorial in Washington DC

TIMELINE

1950	1950	1950
North Korea invades South Korea on June 25, starting the Korean War.	Seoul, South Korea, falls to the North Koreans on June 27.	On July 1, the first US troops land in Korea as part of Task Force Smith and are defeated by North Korean troops on July 5.

1950	1950	1950
On September 15, General Douglas MacArthur lands US forces at Inchon.	On September 16, UN forces begin breaking through the Pusan Perimeter.	On September 25, UN forces arrive in Seoul to take the city from North Korea.

1950

On July 12, the Eighth US Army, commanded by General Walton Walker, takes charge of ground operations in Korea.

1950

On August 1, UN forces establish a defense line around Pusan called the Pusan Perimeter.

1950

Battles of Naktong Bulge and continuous fighting around the perimeter occur between August 5 and September 15.

1950

Chinese forces begin crossing the Yalu River into North Korea on October 14.

1950

US forces take Pyongyang, the North Korean capital, on October 20.

1950

Chinese forces around Unsan crush UN troops in early November.

TIMELINE

1950	1950	1950
On November 21, UN forces continue north; MacArthur says troops will be home by Christmas.	From November 26 to 30, the Chinese defeat UN forces at the Ch'ongch'on River and Chosin Reservoir.	General Walker is killed in a jeep accident on December 23; he is replaced by General Matthew Ridgway.

1951	1951	1951
On April 11, Truman relieves MacArthur of command and replaces him with Ridgway.	On April 22, China begins the first of two spring offensives.	On May 20, UN forces halt the Chinese offensive.

1951

UN forces, having lost Seoul again, establish a defensive line at the 37th parallel in January.

1951

UN forces defeat the Chinese at Chipyongni on February 14.

1951

UN forces retake Seoul on March 18.

1951

On June 13, UN forces are ordered to stop their attack and wait for truce negotiations.

1951

Truce talks begin on July 10, but they stop and start for two years while troops engage in bloody fighting to maintain their current battle lines.

1953

An armistice is signed on July 27.

ESSENTIAL FACTS

DATE OF EVENT

June 25, 1950, to July 27, 1953

PLACE OF EVENT

North Korea and South Korea

KEY PLAYERS

❖ Kim Il Sung, leader of North Korea

❖ Syngman Rhee, leader of South Korea

❖ Joseph Stalin, Soviet premier

❖ Harry S. Truman, US president

❖ Douglas MacArthur, head of US forces in the Far East

❖ Mao Zedong, leader of China

❖ Walton Walker, commander of the Eighth US Army

❖ Matthew Ridgway, MacArthur's successor

HIGHLIGHTS OF EVENT

❖ **June 25, 1950**
North Korea, wanting to unify all Korea under a Communist dictatorship, attacked South Korea without warning.

❖ **June 27, 1950**
The United States, fearing the Soviet Union was behind the North Korean aggression, obtained approval from the United Nations (UN) to authorize military force to protect South Korea.

❖ **July 1, 1950**
The first US troops arrived in Korea. They were later joined by soldiers from other UN member nations. All UN forces were under the command of General Douglas MacArthur.

❖ **July 1950**
In the first month of fighting, UN forces, including South Korean soldiers, were almost driven into the sea by the North Korean army.

❖ **September 15, 1950**
MacArthur's risky and unexpected amphibious landing at Inchon allowed UN forces to storm north past the North Korean border.

❖ **October 14, 1950**
Fearing attack, China sent approximately 300,000 soldiers to help North Korea. The Chinese intervention pushed the UN forces back into South Korea.

❖ **April 11, 1951**
Truman relieved MacArthur of his command and replaced him with Ridgway.

❖ **June 13, 1951**
UN forces were ordered to stop advancing and to hold the line for truce negotiations, which continued off and on for more than two years while fighting proceeded.

❖ **July 27, 1953**
An armistice was signed that ended the war.

Quote

"It was not easy to make the decision to send American boys again [after World War II] into battle. I was a soldier in the First World War, and I know what a soldier goes through. . . . But . . . we realized that the issue was whether there would be fighting in a limited area now or on a much larger scale later on—whether there would be some casualties now or many more casualties later."—*Harry S. Truman, farewell address as president*

GLOSSARY

ambush
A surprise attack.

amphibious
By water and land.

armistice
A temporary stopping of war by mutual agreement.

artillery
Larger firearms, such as missile launchers; they can be mobile or stationary.

casualties
Soldiers lost to service by being killed, wounded, captured, imprisoned, sick, or missing.

cease-fire
A temporary stopping of war by mutual agreement.

communism
A communal economic and political system that stresses workers should control production of economic goods in a society. In a true Communist state, social classes cease to exist, government is unnecessary, and everyone lives in abundance. Today, the term often refers to authoritarian political systems whose leaders claim to advance the rights of the masses, peasants, and workers.

C ration
Canned food issued to soldiers in battle.

flanks
The right and left sides of a battle line.

infantry
Soldiers fighting on the ground.

Joint Chiefs of Staff
A board of advisers to the US president composed of high-ranking members representing each branch of the military as well as a chairman and a vice chairman chosen by the president.

massacre
> A decisive defeat resulting in a large number of dead and wounded.

McCarthyism
> Named for Joseph McCarthy, the act of unfairly accusing someone of being disloyal to the US government, particularly because they are Communist.

morale
> A person's emotional or mental state, particularly when facing challenges.

negotiate
> To bargain or deal; to work out a disagreement through discussion rather than through violence and coercion.

offensive
> On the attack.

perimeter
> A defensive battle line organized around a military position.

propaganda
> Communications designed to persuade people to accept a certain point of view.

reservoir
> A place where water is collected.

retreat
> To withdraw or move back to safer areas.

stalemate
> A position in which two opponents are unable to move.

trench
> A long ditch deep enough in which to take cover from enemy fire.

ADDITIONAL RESOURCES

SELECTED BIBLIOGRAPHY

Fehrenbach, T. R. *This Kind of War: The Classic Korean War History*. Washington, DC: Potomac, 1994. Print.

Hickey, Michael. *The Korean War: The West Confronts Communism*. Woodstock, NY: Overlook, 1999. Print.

MacDonald, Callum A. *Korea: The War Before Vietnam*. New York: Free Press, 1986. Print.

FURTHER READINGS

Goldstein, Donald M., and Harry J. Maihafer. *The Korean War: The Story and Photographs*. Dulles, VA: Potomac, 2001. Print.

Halberstam, David. *The Coldest Winter: America and the Korean War*. New York: Hyperion, 2007. Print.

Varhola, Michael J. *Fire and Ice: The Korean War, 1950–1953*. Cambridge, MA: DaCapo, 2000. Print.

WEB LINKS

To learn more about the Korean War, visit ABDO Publishing Company online at **www.abdopublishing.com**. Web sites about the Korean War are featured on our Book Links page. These links are routinely monitored and updated to provide the most current information available.

Places to Visit

Denis J. Healy Freedom Center for the Korean War National Museum
9 South Old State Capitol Plaza, Springfield IL 62705
888-295-7212
www.theforgottenvictory.org
This is the first museum in the United States dedicated to
the Korean War. Visitors can explore records, photographs,
3-D-interactive exhibits, a canteen, and educational computer
games. Veterans and their families may also record their personal
experiences.

Korean War Memorial
8 YongSan-dong I(il)ga YongSan-Gu, Seoul, Korea 140-021
82-2-709-3139, 3114
www.warmemo.or.kr/eng/intro/message/message.jsp
This memorial has more than 9,000 artifacts from wars in Korea
that range from ancient times through the Korean War. One of
its six exhibit rooms is devoted to the Korean War, and a statue
commemorates the millions of Korean families separated by the
war. In a park outside the memorial, visitors can see planes and
tanks used in the Korean War. The memorial offers information
about the war from the South Korean point of view.

Korean War Veterans Memorial
National Mall and Memorial Parks, 900 Ohio Drive Southwest
Washington, DC 20024
202-426-6841
www.nps.gov/kowa
Statues commemorate the members of all branches of the US
armed forces who served and died in Korea. Inscriptions display
statistics of the Americans who were killed, wounded, captured, or
missing.

Source Notes

Chapter 1. Task Force Smith

1. T. R. Fehrenbach. *This Kind of War*. Washington, DC: Potomac, 1994. Print. 66.

Chapter 2. Why Korea?

1. Dean Acheson. *Present at the Creation*. New York: Norton, 1969. Print. 357.

Chapter 3. Backs against the Sea

1. T. R. Fehrenbach. *This Kind of War*. Washington, DC: Potomac, 1994. Print. 65.

2. "The President's News Conference of June 29, 1950." TeachingAmericanHistory.org. Ashbrook Center for Public Affairs, 2008. Web. 7 Nov. 2010.

3. Ibid.

4. Sundstrom, Carl-Johan. "The Chinese People Cannot Be Cowed by the Atom Bomb." *Selected Works of Mao Tse-tung*. Marxists. org, 2004. Web. 10 Oct. 2010.

5. David Halberstam. "Only a Few Came Home." *Parade*. Parade, 2010. Web. 7 Nov. 2010.

6. T. R. Fehrenbach. *This Kind of War*. Washington, DC: Potomac, 1994. Print. 147.

Chapter 4. MacArthur's Finest Hour

1. "Collections Archive—Focus on the Korean War Era." *History & Collections*. Women in Military Service for America Memorial Foundation, Inc., n.d. Web. 7 Nov. 2010.

2. William H. Warren Sr. "Testimonials: Vignettes from Korean War Veterans (S-Z)." *Virginian-Pilot*. PilotOnline.com, 25 June 2010. Web. 6 Nov. 2010.

Chapter 5. The Road to a Nightmare

1. David Halberstam. *The Coldest Winter*. New York: Hyperion, 2007. Print. 364.

2. Ibid. 365.

3. Ibid. 367.

4. Poise Lee Starkey. "Testimonials: Vignettes from Korean War Veterans (S–Z)." *Virginian–Pilot*. PilotOnline.com, 25 June 2010. Web. 6 Nov. 2010.

Chapter 6. MacArthur's Blindness

1. James Brady. *The Coldest War: A Memoir of Korea*. New York: Tomas Dunne/St. Martin's, 1990. Print. 87.

2. Carl. F. Ullrich. "Testimonials: Vignettes from Korean War Veterans (S–Z)." *Virginian–Pilot*. PilotOnline.com, 25 June 2010. Web. 6 Nov. 2010.

3. Vik Jolly. "Marine: 'First Night We Stacked 700 Bodies.'" *Orange County Register*. Orange County Register Communications, 16 Sept. 2010. Web. 4 Nov. 2010.

Chapter 7. Comeback

1. Marion F. Sturkey. "Code of Conduct." *Warrior Culture of the U.S. Marines*. 2001. Heritage Press International, n.d. Web. 10 Oct. 2010.

2. Michael Hickey. *The Korean War*. Woodstock, New York: Overlook, 1999. Print. 167.

3. T. R. Fehrenbach. *This Kind of War*. Washington, DC: Potomac, 1994. Print. 259.

4. "Collections Archive—Focus on the Korean War Era." *History & Collections*. Women in Military Service for America Memorial Foundation, Inc., n.d. Web. 7 Nov. 2010.

Source Notes Continued

Chapter 8. The Old Soldier Returns Home

1. T. R. Fehrenbach. *This Kind of War*. Washington, DC: Potomac, 1994. Print. 279.

2. Ibid. 282.

3. Ibid. 283.

4. Harry S. Truman. "Speech Explaining the Firing of MacArthur." *TeachingAmericanHistory.org*. Ashbrook Center for Public Affairs, 2008. Web. 10 Oct. 2010.

5. Merle Miller. *Plain Speaking: An Oral Biography of Harry Truman*. New York: Black Dog & Leventhal, 2005. Print. 247.

6. Douglas MacArthur. "Old Soldiers Never Die." *PBS.org: American Experience*. WGBH Educational Foundation, 2006. Web. 10 Oct. 2010.

Chapter 9. Stalemate

1. Betty A. Williams. "Testimonials: Vignettes from Korean War Veterans (S-Z)." *Virginian-Pilot*. PilotOnline.com, 25 June 2010. Web. 6 Nov. 2010.

2. Harry S. Truman. "The President's Farewell Address to the American People." *Truman Library: Public Papers*. Harry S. Truman Library & Museum, n.d. Web. 10 Oct. 2010.

Chapter 10. The Forgotten War

1. Carl. F. Ullrich. "Testimonials: Vignettes from Korean War Veterans (S-Z)." *Virginian-Pilot*. PilotOnline.com, 25 June 2010. Web. 6 Nov. 2010.

2. Amber Nicholson. "Veterans Remember Forgotten War." *Journal Pioneer*. Transcontinental Media, 25 June 2010. Web. 6 Nov. 2010.

Index

INDEX CONTINUED

About the Author

Richard Reece is a longtime magazine editor and a writer of fiction and nonfiction. A native of Kansas City, Missouri, he grew up in Minnesota where he worked as a middle school teacher for several years. He now resides in Raleigh, North Carolina, with his children.

Photo Credits